Holiday itty bitties ™

General Information

Many of the products used in this pattern book can be purchased from local craft, fabric and variety stores, or from the Annie's Attic Needlecraft Catalog (see Customer Service information on page 40).

Contents

2 Santa Claus

6 Mrs. Santa

11 Elf

15 Reindeer

18 Snowman

22 Pilgrim Girl

25 Pilgrim Boy

30 Easter Bunny

34 Uncle Sam

38 Stitch Guide

39 Metric Conversion Charts

Santa Claus

SKILL LEVEL

EASY

FINISHED SIZE
Fits 5-inch doll

MATERIALS
- Aunt Lydia's Classic Crochet size 10 crochet cotton (white: 400 yds per ball; solids: 350 yds per ball):
  - 1 ball each #494 victory red, #1 white, #12 black, #131 fudge brown and #484 myrtle green
- Size 7/1.65mm steel crochet hook or size needed to obtain gauge
- Tapestry needle
- Sewing needle
- 5mm snaps: 2
- ¼-inch white pompom
- White and red sewing thread
- Stitch marker

GAUGE
9 sc = 1 inch

PATTERN NOTES
Join with slip stitch as indicated unless otherwise stated.

Chain-3 at beginning of round counts as first double crochet unless otherwise stated.

INSTRUCTIONS
JACKET
Row 1: Starting at **neck**, with victory red, ch 29, 2 sc in 2nd ch from hook and in each ch across, turn. *(56 sc)*

Row 2: Ch 1, sc in each st across, turn.

Row 3: Ch 1, hdc in each of first 8 sts, for **armhole**, ch 8, sk next 12 sts, hdc in each of next 16 sts, for **armhole**, ch 8, sk next 12 sts, hdc in each of last 8 sts, turn. *(32 hdc, 16 chs)*

Row 4: Ch 1, hdc in each of first 8 sts, sc in each of next 8 chs, hdc in each of next 16 sts, sc in each of next 8 chs, hdc in each of last 8 sts, turn. *(48 sts)*

Row 5: Ch 1, hdc in each of first 8 sts, sc in each of next 8 sts, hdc in each of next 16 sts, sc in each of next 8 sts, hdc in each of last 8 sts, turn.

Rows 6 & 7: Ch 1, sc in each st across, turn. Fasten off at end of last row. *(48 sc)*

Row 8: **Join** *(see Pattern Notes)* black in first st, ch 1, hdc in same st and in each st across, turn. Fasten off.

Row 9: Join victory red with sc in first st, sc in each st across, turn.

Rows 10–13: Ch 1, sc in each st across, turn. Fasten off at end of last row.

TRIM
Row 1: Join white with sc in top of left front at neck edge, working in ends of rows and sts around fronts and bottom edge, evenly sp sc around to top right front at neck edge with 3 sc in each corner, turn.

Row 2: Ch 1, sc in each st across with 3 in each center corner st, **do not turn**.

COLLAR
Row 1: 3 sc in end of row 1 on Trim, working in starting ch on opposite side of row 1 on Jacket, sc in each ch across neck edge, 2 in end of row 1 on Trim, turn. *(33 sc)*

Row 2: Working this row in **front lps** *(see Stitch Guide)*, ch 3, dc in same st, 2 dc in each st across, ch 3, sl st in same st as last st. Fasten off.

SLEEVES

Rnd 1: Join victory red with sc at base of 1 armhole, evenly sp 21 sc around, join with in beg sc. *(22 sc)*

Rnd 2: Ch 1, sc in each of first 11 sts, sk next st, **sc dec** *(see Stitch Guide)* in next 2 sts, sc in each of next 5 sts, sc dec in next 2 sts, sc in last st, join in beg sc. *(19 sc)*

Rnds 3–9: Ch 1, sc in each st around, join in beg sc. Fasten off at end of last rnd.

Rnd 10: Join white with sc in first st, sc in each st around, join in beg sc.

Rnd 11: Ch 1, sc in each st around, join in beg sc. Fasten off.

Rep on other armhole.

Sew 2 snaps evenly sp down front opening.

PANTS

Rnd 1: With victory red, ch 38, join in beg ch to form ring, ch 1, sc in first ch and in each ch around, join in beg sc. *(38 sc)*

Rnds 2–9: Ch 1, sc in each st around, join in beg sc.

FIRST LEG

Rnd 1: Ch 5, sk first 19 sts, sc in each of next 19 sts, sc in each of first 5 chs, join in beg sc. *(24 sc)*

Rnds 2–8: Ch 1, sc in each st around, join in beg sc. Fasten off at end of last rnd.

Rnd 9: Join white with sc in first st, sc in each st around, join in beg sc.

Rnd 10: Ch 1, sc in each st around, join in beg sc. Fasten off.

2ND LEG

Rnd 1: Working on opposite side of ch-5, join white with sc in first ch, sc in each of next

4 chs, sc in each of next 19 skipped sts on rnd 9 of Pants, join in beg sc. *(24 sc)*

Rnds 2–10: Rep rnds 2–10 of First Leg.

BOOT
MAKE 2.

Rnd 1: With black, ch 8, 2 sc in 2nd ch from hook, sc in each of next 4 chs, hdc in next ch, 4 hdc in last ch, working on opposite side of ch, hdc in next ch, sc in each of next 4 chs, 2 sc in last ch, join in beg sc. *(18 sts)*

Rnd 2: Ch 1, 2 sc in first st, sc in each of next 5 sts, hdc in next st, 2 hdc in each of next 4 sts, hdc in next st, sc in each of next 5 sts, 2 sc in last st, join in beg sc. *(24 sts)*

Rnd 3: Working this rnd in **back lps** *(see Stitch Guide)*, ch 1, sc in each st around, join in beg sc. *(24 sc)*

Rnd 4: Ch 1, sc in each st around, join in beg sc.

Rnd 5: Ch 1, sc in each of first 8 sts, [**hdc dec** *(see Stitch Guide)* in next 2 sts] 4 times, sc in each of last 8 sts, join in beg sc. *(20 sts)*

Rnd 6: Ch 1, sc in each of first 8 sts, [hdc dec in next 2 sts] twice, sc in each of last 8 sts, join in beg sc. *(18 sts)*

Rnd 7: Ch 1, sc in each of first 7 sts, [sc dec in next 2 sts] twice, sc in each of last 7 sts, join in beg sc. *(16 sc)*

Rnds 8 & 9: Ch 1, sc in each st around, join in beg sc. Fasten off at end of last rnd.

HAT

Rnd 1: Starting at **cuff**, with white, ch 42, join in beg ch to form ring, ch 1, sc in each ch around, join in beg sc. *(42 sc)*

Rnd 2: Ch 1, sc in each st around, join in beg sc. Fasten off.

Rnd 3: Join victory red with sc in first st, sc in each st around, join in beg sc.

Rnds 4–8: Ch 1, sc in each st around, join in beg sc.

Rnd 9: Ch 1, sc in each of first 19 sts, sc dec in next 2 sts, sc in each of next 19 sts sc dec in last 2 sts, join in beg sc. *(40 sc)*

Rnd 10: Ch 1, sc in each st around, join in beg sc.

Rnd 11: Ch 1, sc in each of first 8 sts, sc dec in next 2 sts, [sc in each of next 8 sts, sc dec in next 2 sts] around, join in beg sc. *(36 sc)*

Rnd 12: Ch 1, sc in each st around, join in beg sc.

Rnd 13: Ch 1, sc in each of first 7 sts, sc dec in next 2 sts, [sc in each of next 7 sts, sc dec in next 2 sts] around, join in beg sc. *(32 sc)*

Rnd 14: Ch 1, sc in each st around, join in beg sc.

Rnd 15: Ch 1, sc in each of first 6 sts, sc dec in next 2 sts, [sc in each of next 6 sts, sc dec in next 2 sts] around, join in beg sc. *(28 sc)*

Rnd 16: Ch 1, sc in each of first 5 sts, sc dec in next 2 sts, [sc in each of next 5 sts, sc dec in next 2 sts] around, join in beg sc. *(24 sc)*

Rnd 17: Ch 1, sc in each of first 4 sts, sc dec in next 2 sts, [sc in each of next 4 sts, sc dec in next 2 sts] around, join in beg sc. *(20 sc)*

Rnd 18: Ch 1, sc in each of first 3 sts, sc dec in next 2 sts, [sc in each of next 3 sts, sc dec in next 2 sts] around, join in beg sc. *(16 sc)*

Rnd 19: Ch 1, sc in each of first 2 sts, sc dec in next 2 sts, [sc in each of next 2 sts, sc dec in next 2 sts] around, join in beg sc. *(12 sc)*

Rnd 20: Ch 1, sc in each of first 4 sts, sc dec in next 2 sts, sc in each of next 4 sts, sc dec in last 2 sts, join in beg sc. *(10 sc)*

Rnd 21: Ch 1, sc in each of first 3 sts, sc dec in next 2 sts, sc in each of next 3 sts, sc dec in last 2 sts, join in beg sc. *(8 sc)*

Rnd 22: Ch 1, sc in each of first 2 sts, sc dec in next 2 sts, sc in each of next 2 sts, sc dec in last 2 sts, join in beg sc. Fasten off. *(6 sc)*

Sew pompom to tip of Hat.

MITTEN
MAKE 2.
Rnd 1: With myrtle green, ch 2, 6 sc in 2nd ch from hook, **do not join.** *(6 sc)*

Note: Do not join or turn rem rnds unless otherwise stated. Mark first st of each rnd.

Rnd 2: 2 sc in each st around. *(12 sc)*

Rnd 3: [Sc in each of next 2 sts, 2 sc in next st] around. *(16 sc)*

Rnd 4: [Sc in each of next 7 sts, 2 sc in next st] around. *(18 sc)*

Rnd 5: Sc in each st around.

Rnd 6: For **thumb**, ch 4, 2 hdc in 3rd ch from hook, hdc in next ch, sc in each of next 18 sts. *(18 sc, 3 hdc)*

Rnd 7: Sk thumb, [sc in each of next 7 sts, sc dec in next 2 sts] around. *(16 sc)*

Rnd 8: [Sc in each of next 6 sts, sc dec in next 2 sts] around. *(14 sc)*

Rnd 9: Sc in each st around.

Rnd 10: Sc in each st around, join in beg sc. Fasten off.

SACK
Rnd 1: With fudge brown, ch 6, dc in 3rd ch from hook, dc in each of next 2 chs, 3 dc in last ch, working on opposite side of ch, dc in each of next 3 chs, 3 dc in next ch, join in top of beg dc. *(12 dc)*

Rnd 2: Ch 3 *(see Pattern Notes)*, dc in same st, 2 dc in each st around, join in 3rd ch of beg ch-3. *(24 dc)*

Rnd 3: Ch 3, 2 dc in next st, [dc in next st, 2 dc in next st] around, join in 3rd ch of beg ch-3. *(36 dc)*

Rnd 4: Ch 3, dc in next st, 2 dc in next st, [dc in each of next 2 sts, 2 dc in next st] around, join in 3rd ch of beg ch-3. *(48 dc)*

Rnds 5–11: Ch 3, dc in each st around, join in 3rd ch of beg ch-3.

Rnd 12: Ch 4 *(counts as first dc and ch-1 sp)*, sk next st, [dc in next st, ch 1, sk next st] around, join in 3rd ch of beg ch-4. *(24 dc, 24 ch sps)*

Rnd 13: Ch 1, sc in first st, sc in each st and in each ch sp around, join in beg sc. Fasten off.

DRAWSTRING
With fudge brown, ch 65. Fasten off.

Weave through sts of rnd 12, tie ends tog.

PATCH
Row 1: With victory red, ch 6, sc in 2nd ch from hook and in each ch across, turn. *(5 sc)*

Rows 2–5: Ch 1, sc in each st across, turn. Fasten off at end of last row.

Sew to 1 side of Sack. ∎

Mrs. Santa

FINISHED SIZE
Fits 5-inch doll

MATERIALS
- Aunt Lydia's Classic Crochet size 10 crochet cotton (white: 400 yds per ball; solids: 350 yds per ball):
    1 ball each #494 victory red, #1 white, #12 black, #131 fudge brown, #310 copper mist and #484 myrtle green
- Size 7/1.65mm steel crochet hook or size needed to obtain gauge
- Sewing needle
- ¼ yd black embroidery floss
- 5mm snap: 1
- 10 red seed beads
- White and red sewing thread

GAUGE
9 sc = 1 inch

PATTERN NOTES
Join with slip stitch as indicated unless otherwise stated.

Chain-3 at beginning of round counts as first double crochet unless otherwise stated.

SPECIAL STITCHES
Shell: 7 dc in next st.

Picot: Ch 3, sl st in side of last st made.

INSTRUCTIONS
DRESS
Row 1: Starting at **bodice**, with victory red, ch 29, 2 sc in 2nd ch from hook and in each ch across, turn. *(56 sc)*

Row 2: Ch 1, sc in each st across, turn.

Row 3: Ch 1, hdc in each of first 8 sts, for **armhole**, ch 8, sk next 12 sts, hdc in each of next 16 sts, for **armhole**, ch 8, sk next 12 sts, hdc in each of last 8 sts, turn. *(32 hdc, 16 chs)*

Row 4: Ch 1, hdc in each of first 8 sts, sc in each of next 8 chs, hdc in each of next 16 sts, sc in each of next 8 chs, hdc in each of last 8 sts, turn. *(48 sts)*

Row 5: Ch 1, hdc in each of first 8 sts, sc in each of next 8 sts, hdc in each of next 16 sts, sc in each of next 8 sts, hdc in each of last 8 sts, turn.

Row 6: Ch 1, sc in each st across, turn. *(48 sc)*

Rnd 7: Now working in rounds, for **skirt, ch 3** *(see Pattern Notes)*, 6 dc in same st, sk next st, sc in next st, sk next st, [**shell** *(see Special Stitches)* in next st, sk next st, sc in next st, sk next st] around, **join** *(see Pattern Notes)* in 3rd ch of beg ch-3. *(12 shells, 12 sc)*

Rnd 8: Sl st in each of next 3 sts, ch 1, sc in same st as last sl st, ch 1, shell in next sc, ch 1, [sc in center st of next shell, ch 1, shell in next sc, ch 1] around, join in beg sc.

Rnd 9: Ch 3, 6 dc in same st, ch 1, sc in center st of next shell, ch 1, [shell in next sc, ch 1, sc in center st of next shell, ch 1] around, join in 3rd ch of beg ch-3.

Rnds 10–13: [Rep rnds 8 and 9] twice.

Rnd 14: Rep rnd 8. Fasten off.

SLEEVES
Rnd 1: Join victory red with sc at base of 1 armhole, evenly sp 21 sc around, join with in beg sc. *(22 sc)*

Rnd 2: Ch 1, sc in each of first 12 sts, **sc dec** (see Stitch Guide) in next 2 sts, sc in each of next 5 sts, sc dec in next 2 sts, sc in last st, join in beg sc. (20 sc)

Rnd 3: Ch 1, sc in first st, sk next st, 3 dc in next st, sk next st, [sc in next st, sk next st, 3 dc in next st, sk next st] around, join in beg sc. (5 3-dc groups, 5 sc)

Rnd 4: Ch 3, 2 dc in same st, sk next st, sc in next st, sk next st, [3 dc in next st, sk next st, sc in next st, sk next st] around, join in 3rd ch of beg ch-3.

Rnd 5: Sl st in next st, ch 1, sc in same st, sk next st, 3 dc in next st, sk next st, [sc in next st, sk next st, 3 dc in next st, sk next st] around, join in beg sc.

Rnds 6 & 7: Rep rnds 4 and 5. Fasten off at end of last rnd.

Rnd 8: For **trim**, join white with sc in first st, **picot** (see Special Stitches), sk next st, *(sc, picot) in next st, sk next st, rep from * around, join in beg sc. Fasten off.

Rep on other armhole.

COLLAR
Working in starting ch on opposite side of row 1 on bodice at neck edge, join white with sc in first ch, [ch 2, sc in next ch] across. Fasten off.

Sew snap to back opening.

APRON
BIB
Row 1: With white, ch 9, sc in 2nd ch from hook and in each ch across, turn. (8 sc)

Row 2: Ch 1, sc in each st across, turn.

Row 3: Ch 1, sc in first st, [ch 2, sc in next st] across, for **neck tie**, ch 45. Fasten off.

For **2nd neck tie**, join white in st on opposite end of row 3, ch 45. Fasten off.

SKIRT
Row 1: With white, ch 17, working in starting ch on opposite side of row 1 on Bib, join with sc in first ch, sc in each ch across, turn. (8 sc, 1 ch-17)

Row 2: Ch 18, sc in 2nd ch from hook and in each of next 16 chs, sc in each of next 8 sts, sc in each ch of ch-17, turn. (42 sc)

Row 3: Ch 1, hdc in each of first 2 sts, 2 hdc in next st, [hdc in each of next 2 sts, 2 hdc in next st] across, turn. (56 hdc)

Rows 4–9: Ch 1, hdc in each st across, turn.

Row 10: Ch 1, sc in first st, [ch 2, sc in next st] across. Fasten off.

For **waist tie**, join white in end of row 1 on Skirt, ch 35. Fasten off. Rep on opposite side of row 1.

LEAF
MAKE 2.
With myrtle green, ch 5, sl st in 2nd ch from hook, sl st in next ch, ch 2, sl st in 2nd ch from hook, sl st in next ch, (sl st, {ch 2, sl st in 2nd ch from hook} twice, sl st) in last ch, working on opposite side of ch, sl st in next ch, ch 2, sl st in 2nd ch from hook, sl st in each of last 2 chs. Fasten off.

Sew 5 beads in a cluster to center front of Bib, Sew 1 Leaf to each side of beads.

HAT
Rnd 1: Ch 4, join in beg ch to form ring, ch 3, 11 dc in ring, join in 3rd ch of beg ch-3. *(12 dc)*

Rnd 2: Ch 3, dc in same st, 2 dc in each st around, join in 3rd ch of beg ch-3. *(24 dc)*

Rnd 3: Ch 3, 2 dc in next st, [dc in next st, 2 dc in next st] around, join in 3rd ch of beg ch-3. *(36 dc)*

Rnd 4: Ch 2, dc in next st, 2 dc in next st, [dc in each of next 2 sts, 2 dc in next st] around, join in 3rd ch of beg ch-3. *(48 dc)*

Rnd 5: Ch 3, dc in each of next 2 sts, 2 dc in next st, [dc in each of next 3 sts, 2 dc in next st] around, join in 3rd ch of beg ch-3. *(60 dc)*

Rnd 6: Ch 3, dc in each st around, join in 3rd ch of beg ch-3.

Rnd 7: For **ruffle**, ch 1, **sc dec** *(see Stitch Guide)* in first 2 sts, sc dec in next 2 sts, sk next st, *[sc dec in next 2 sts] twice, sk next st, rep from * around, join in beg sc. *(24 sc)*

Rnd 8: Ch 3, 4 dc in same st, 5 dc in each st around, join in 3rd ch of beg ch-3. Fasten off.

LEAF
MAKE 2.
Work same as Apron Leaf.

Sew 5 beads in a cluster to Hat above ruffle. Sew one Leaf to each side of beads.

BLOOMERS
Rnd 1: With white, ch 38, join in beg ch to form ring, ch 1, sc in first ch and in each ch around, join in beg sc. *(38 sc)*

Rnds 2–9: Ch 1, sc in each st around, join in beg sc.

FIRST LEG
Rnd 1: Ch 5, sk first 19 sts, sc in each of next 19 sts, sc in each of first 5 chs, join in beg sc. *(24 sc)*

Rnds 2–9: Ch 1, sc in each st around, join in beg sc.

Rnd 10: Ch 1, sc in first st, ch 2, [sc in next st, ch 2] around, join in beg sc. Fasten off.

2ND LEG
Rnd 1: Working on opposite side of ch-5, join white with sc in first ch, sc in each of next 4 chs, sc in each of next 19 skipped sts on rnd 9 of Bloomers, join in beg sc. *(24 sc)*

Rnds 2–10: Rep rnds 2–10 of First Leg.

BOOT
MAKE 2.
Rnd 1: With black, ch 8, 2 sc in 2nd ch from hook, sc in each of next 4 chs, hdc in next ch, 4 hdc in last ch, working on opposite side of ch, hdc in next ch, sc in each of next 4 chs, 2 sc in last ch, join in beg sc. *(18 sts)*

Rnd 2: Ch 1, 2 sc in first st, sc in each of next 5 sts, hdc in next st, 2 hdc in each of next 4 sts, hdc in next st, sc in each of next 5 sts, 2 sc in last st, join in beg sc. *(24 sts)*

Rnd 3: Working this rnd in **back lps** *(see Stitch Guide)*, ch 1, sc in each st around, join in beg sc. *(24 sc)*

Rnd 4: Ch 1, sc in each st around, join in beg sc.

Rnd 5: Ch 1, sc in each of first 8 sts, [**hdc dec** *(see Stitch Guide)* in next 2 sts] 4 times, sc in each of last 8 sts, join in beg sc. *(20 sts)*

Rnd 6: Ch 1, sc in each of first 8 sts, [hdc dec in next 2 sts] twice, sc in each of last 8 sts, join in beg sc. *(18 sts)*

Rnd 7: Ch 1, sc in each of first 7 sts, [sc dec in next 2 sts] twice, sc in each of last 7 sts, join in beg sc. *(16 sc)*

Rnds 8 & 9: Ch 1, sc in each st around, join in beg sc. Fasten off at end of last rnd.

BASKET
Rnd 1: Starting at bottom, with fudge brown, ch 8, sc in 2nd ch from hook and in each of next 5 chs, 3 sc in last ch, working on opposite side of ch, sc in each of next 5 chs, 2 sc in same ch as beg sc, join in beg sc. *(16 sc)*

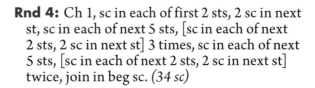

Rnd 2: Ch 1, 2 sc in first st, sc in each of next 5 sts, 2 sc in each of next 3 sts, sc in each of next 5 sts, 2 sc in each of last 2 sts, join in beg sc. *(22 sc)*

Rnd 3: Ch 1, sc in first st, 2 sc in next st, sc in each of next 5 sts, [sc in next st, 2 sc in next st] 3 times, sc in each of next 5 sts, [sc in next st, 2 sc in next st] twice, join in beg sc. *(28 sc)*

Rnd 4: Ch 1, sc in each of first 2 sts, 2 sc in next st, sc in each of next 5 sts, [sc in each of next 2 sts, 2 sc in next st] 3 times, sc in each of next 5 sts, [sc in each of next 2 sts, 2 sc in next st] twice, join in beg sc. *(34 sc)*

Rnd 5: Working this rnd in back lps, ch 1, sc in each st around, join in beg sc.

Rnd 6: Ch 1, sc in each st around, join in beg sc.

Rnd 7: Ch 1, sc in each of first 15 sts, sc dec in next 2 sts, sc in each of next 15 sts, sc dec in last 2 sts, join in beg sc. *(32 sc)*

Rnd 8: Ch 1, sc in each st around, join in beg sc.

Rnd 9: Ch 2 *(counts as first hdc)*, 4 hdc in same st, sk next st, sc in next st, sk next st, [5 hdc in next st, sk next st, sc in next st, sk next st] around, join in 2nd ch of beg ch-2. Fasten off.

HANDLE
With fudge brown, ch 20, sc in 2nd ch from hook and in each ch across. Fasten off.

Sew 1 Handle end to each side of Basket on inside *(see photo)*.

GINGERBREAD MAN COOKIE
MAKE 2.
Rnd 1: Starting at **head**, with copper mist, ch 2, 7 sc in 2nd ch from hook, **do not join**. *(7 sc)*

Rnd 2: 2 sc in each st around, join in beg sc. *(14 sc)*

Row 3: Now working in rows for **body**, ch 1, 2 sc in each of first 2 sts, leaving rem sts unworked, turn. *(4 sc)*

Rows 4 & 5: For **arm**, ch 5, hdc in 3rd ch from hook and in each of next 2 chs, sc in each of next 4 sts, turn.

Row 6: Ch 1, sc in each of first 4 sts, leaving arm unworked, turn.

Row 7: For **legs,** [ch 6, hdc in 3rd ch from hook, hdc in each of next 3 chs, sk next sc, sc in next sc] twice. Fasten off.

FINISHING

1. With 3 strands embroidery floss, using **satin stitch** *(see Fig. 1)*, embroider eyes to head ⅛ inch apart.

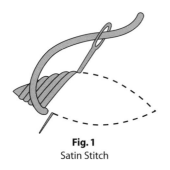

Fig. 1
Satin Stitch

2. With 3 strands floss, using **straight stitch** *(see Fig. 2)*, embroider mouth centered below eyes on Head and 2 buttons down center front of body *(see photo)*.

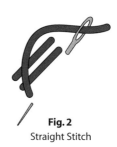

Fig. 2
Straight Stitch

3. With white, using **chain stitch** *(see Fig. 3)*, embroider around entire outside edge of Gingerbread Man Cookie. ∎

Fig. 3
Chain Stitch

Elf

SKILL LEVEL

EASY

FINISHED SIZE
Fits 5-inch doll

MATERIALS
- Aunt Lydia's Classic Crochet size 10 crochet cotton (350 yds per ball):
  1 ball each #397 wasabi, #12 black, #421 goldenrod and #484 myrtle green
- Size 7/1.65mm steel crochet hook or size needed to obtain gauge
- Sewing needle
- 5mm snaps: 2
- Polyester fiberfill
- Green sewing thread

GAUGE
9 sc = 1 inch

PATTERN NOTE
Join with slip stitch as indicated unless otherwise stated.

SPECIAL STITCH
Cluster (cl): Yo, insert hook in 3rd ch from hook, yo, pull lp through, yo, pull through 2 lps on hook, [yo, insert hook in same ch, yo, pull lp through, yo, pull through 2 lps on hook] twice, yo, pull through all 4 lps on hook.

INSTRUCTIONS
TUNIC
Row 1 (RS): Starting at **neck**, with myrtle green, ch 29, 2 sc in 2nd ch from hook and in each ch across, turn. (*56 sc*)

Row 2: Ch 1, sc in each st across, turn.

Row 3: Ch 1, hdc in each of first 8 sts, for **armhole**, ch 8, sk next 12 sts, hdc in each of next 16 sts, for **armhole**, ch 8, sk next 12 sts, hdc in each of last 8 sts, turn. (*32 hdc, 16 chs*)

Row 4: Ch 1, hdc in each of first 8 sts, sc in each of next 8 chs, hdc in each of next 16 sts, sc in each of next 8 chs, hdc in each of last 8 sts, turn. (*48 sts*)

Row 5: Ch 1, hdc in each of first 8 sts, sc in each of next 8 sts, hdc in each of next 16 sts, sc in each of next 8 sts, hdc in each of last 8 sts, turn.

Rows 6 & 7: Ch 1, sc in each st across, turn. Fasten off at end of last row.

Row 8: **Join** *(see Pattern Note)* black in first st, ch 1, hdc in same st and in each st across, turn. Fasten off.

Row 9: Join myrtle green with sc in first st, sc in each st across, turn.

Rows 10–11: Ch 1, sc in each st across, turn.

Row 12: Ch 1, sc in each of first 4 sts, *turn, [sc **dec** *(see Stitch Guide)* in next 2 sts] twice, **turn**, ch 1, sc in each of next 2 sts, **turn**, ch 1, sc dec in next 2 sts, **turn**, ch 1, sc in next st, sl st in end of each of next 3 rows, sl st in same st on row 11 as last st**, sc in each of next 4 sts on row 11, rep from * across, ending last rep at **. Fasten off.

COLLAR
Row 1: With WS facing, working in starting ch on opposite side of row 1, join wasabi with sc in first ch, sc in each ch across, turn. *(28 sc)*

Row 2: Working this row in **front lps** *(see Stitch Guide)*, ch 1, sc in first st, 2 sc in next st, [sc in next st, 2 sc in next st] across, turn. *(42 sc)*

Row 3: Ch 1, sk first st, sl st in each of next 2 sts, [ch 4, sl st in 2nd ch from hook, sc in next ch, hdc in next ch, sk next st, sl st each of next 2 sts] across. Fasten off.

SLEEVES
Rnd 1: Join myrtle green with sc at base of 1 armhole, evenly sp 21 sc around, join with in beg sc. *(22 sc)*

Rnd 2: Ch 1, sc in each of first 11 sts, sk next st, **sc dec** *(see Stitch Guide)* in next 2 sts, sc in each of next 5 sts, sc dec in next 2 sts, sc in last st, join in beg sc. *(19 sc)*

Rnds 3–9: Ch 1, sc in each st around, join in beg sc. Fasten off at end of last row.

Rnd 10: Join wasabi with sc in first st, sc in each st around, join in beg sc.

Rnd 11: Ch 1, sc in each st around, join in beg sc. Fasten off.

Rep on other armhole.

Sew 2 snaps evenly sp down back opening.

With goldenrod, using **straight stitch** *(see Fig. 1)*, embroider a square over center front of row 8 for **belt buckle**.

Fig. 1
Straight Stitch

PANTS
Rnd 1: With wasabi, ch 38, join in beg ch to form ring, ch 1, sc in first ch and in each ch around, join in beg sc. *(38 sc)*

Rnds 2–9: Ch 1, sc in each st around, join in beg sc.

FIRST LEG
Rnd 1: Ch 5, sk first 19 sts, sc in each of next 19 sts, sc in each of first 5 chs, join in beg sc. *(24 sc)*

Rnds 2–4: Ch 1, sc in each st around, join in beg sc.

Rnd 5: Ch 1, sc in each of first 6 sts, sc dec in next 2 sts, [sc in each of next 6 sts, sc dec in next 2 sts] around, join in beg sc. *(21 sc)*

Rnds 6–9: Ch 1, sc in each st around, join in beg sc. Fasten off at end of last rnd.

2ND LEG
Rnd 1: Working on opposite side of ch-5, join wasabi with sc in first ch, sc in each of next 4 chs, sc in each of next 19 unworked sts on rnd 9 of Pants, join in beg sc. *(24 sc)*

Rnds 2–9: Rep rnds 2–9 of First Leg.

BOOTIE
MAKE 2.

Rnd 1: With myrtle green, ch 8, 2 sc in 2nd ch from hook, sc in each of next 4 chs, hdc in next ch, 4 hdc in last ch, working on opposite side of ch, hdc in next ch, sc in each of next 4 chs, 2 sc in last ch, join in beg sc. *(18 sts)*

Rnd 2: Ch 1, 2 sc in first st, sc in each of next 5 sts, hdc in next st, 2 hdc in each of next 4 sts, hdc in next st, sc in each of next 5 sts, 2 sc in last st, join in beg sc. *(24 sts)*

Rnd 3: Working this rnd in **back lps** *(see Stitch Guide)*, ch 1, sc in each st around, join in beg sc. *(24 sc)*

Rnd 4: Ch 1, sc in each st around, join in beg sc.

Rnd 5: Ch 1, sc in each of first 8 sts, [**hdc dec** *(see Stitch Guide)* in next 2 sts] 4 times, sc in each of last 8 sts, join in beg sc. *(20 sts)*

Rnd 6: Ch 1, sc in each of first 8 sts, [hdc dec in next 2 sts] twice, sc in each of last 8 sts, join in beg sc. *(18 sts)*

Rnd 7: Ch 1, sc in each of first 7 sts, [sc dec in next 2 sts] twice, sc in each of last 7 sts, join in beg sc. *(16 sc)*

Rnd 8: Ch 1, sc in each st around, join in beg sc.

Rnd 9: Ch 1, sc in each of first 3 sts, 2 sc in next st, [sc in each of next 3 sts, 2 sc in next st] around, join in beg sc, turn. *(20 sc)*

Rnd 10: Working this rnd in back lps, sc in first st, [ch 2, sc in next st] around, join in beg sc. Fasten off.

BOOTIE TIP

Rnd 1: With myrtle green, ch 2, 6 sc in 2nd ch from hook, **do not join.** *(6 sc)*

Note: Do not join or turn rem rnds unless otherwise stated. Mark first st of each rnd.

Rnd 2: Sc in each st around.

Rnds 3 & 4: Sl st in each of first 3 sts, hdc in each of last 3 sts. *(6 sts)*

Rnd 5: [Sc in next st, 2 sc in next st] around. *(9 sc)*

Rnd 6: Sc in each of next 2 sts, sl st in each of next 3 sts, sc in next st, hdc in each of last 3 sts. *(9 sts)*

Rnd 7: Hdc in next st, sc in next st, sl st in next st, leaving rem sts unworked. Fasten off.

Stuff Bootie Tip with fiberfill and sew to toe of Bootie.

HAT

Rnd 1: Starting at **cuff**, with wasabi, ch 42, join in beg ch to form ring, ch 1, sc in each ch around, join in beg sc, **turn**. *(42 sc)*

Rnd 2: Working this rnd in back lps, ch 1, sk first st, sl st in each of next 2 sts, ch 4, sl st in 2nd ch from hook, sc in next ch, hdc in next ch, [sk next st on rnd 1, sl st each of next 2 sts, ch 4, sl st in 2nd ch from hook, sc in next ch, hdc in next ch] around, join in beg sl st of last rnd. Fasten off.

Rnd 3: Working in starting ch on opposite side of rnd 1, join myrtle green with sc in first st, sc in each st around, join in beg sc. *(42 sc)*

Rnds 4–8: Ch 1, sc in each st around, join in beg sc.

Rnd 9: Ch 1, sc in each of first 19 sts, sc dec in next 2 sts, sc in each of next 19 sts sc dec in last 2 sts, join in beg sc. *(40 sc)*

Rnd 10: Ch 1, sc in each st around, join in beg sc.

Rnd 11: Ch 1, sc in each of first 8 sts, sc dec in next 2 sts, [sc in each of next 8 sts, sc dec in next 2 sts] around, join in beg sc. *(36 sc)*

Rnd 12: Ch 1, sc in each st around, join in beg sc.

Rnd 13: Ch 1, sc in each of first 7 sts, sc dec in next 2 sts, [sc in each of next 7 sts, sc dec in next 2 sts] around, join in beg sc. *(32 sc)*

Rnd 14: Ch 1, sc in each st around, join in beg sc.

Rnd 15: Ch 1, sc in each of first 6 sts, sc dec in next 2 sts, [sc in each of next 6 sts, sc dec in next 2 sts] around, join in beg sc. *(28 sc)*

Rnd 16: Ch 1, sc in each of first 5 sts, sc dec in next 2 sts, [sc in each of next 5 sts, sc dec in next 2 sts] around, join in beg sc. *(24 sc)*

Rnd 17: Ch 1, sc in each of first 4 sts, sc dec in next 2 sts, [sc in each of next 4 sts, sc dec in next 2 sts] around, join in beg sc. *(20 sc)*

Rnd 18: Ch 1, sc in each of first 3 sts, sc dec in next 2 sts, [sc in each of next 3 sts, sc dec in next 2 sts] around, join in beg sc. *(16 sc)*

Rnd 19: Ch 1, sc in each of first 2 sts, sc dec in next 2 sts, [sc in each of next 2 sts, sc dec in next 2 sts] around, join in beg sc. *(12 sc)*

Rnd 20: Ch 1, sc in each of first 4 sts, sc dec in next 2 sts, sc in each of next 4 sts, sc dec in last 2 sts, join in beg sc. *(10 sc)*

Rnd 21: Ch 1, sc in each of first 3 sts, sc dec in next 2 sts, sc in each of next 3 sts, sc dec in last 2 sts, join in beg sc. *(8 sc)*

Rnd 22: Ch 1, sc in each of first 2 sts, sc dec in next 2 sts, sc in each of next 2sts, sc dec in last 2 sts, join in beg sc. Fasten off. *(6 sc)*

POMPOM

With wasabi, ch 3, **cl** *(see Special Stitch)* in 3rd ch from hook. Fasten off.

Sew Pompom to tip of Hat. ■

Reindeer

SKILL LEVEL

EASY

FINISHED SIZE
Fits 5-inch doll

MATERIALS
- Aunt Lydia's Classic Crochet size 10 crochet cotton (350 yds per ball):
  1 ball each #310 copper mist and #420 cream
- Size 7/1.65mm steel crochet hook or size needed to obtain gauge
- Sewing needle
- 5mm snap: 1
- Brown sewing thread

GAUGE
9 sc = 1 inch

PATTERN NOTE
Join with slip stitch as indicated unless otherwise stated.

INSTRUCTIONS
SUIT
Row 1: Starting at **neck**, with copper mist, ch 29, 2 sc in 2nd ch from hook and in each ch across, turn. *(56 sc)*

Row 2: Ch 1, sc in each st across, turn.

Row 3: Ch 1, hdc in each of first 8 sts, for **armhole**, ch 8, sk next 12 sts, hdc in each of next 16 sts, for **armhole**, ch 8, sk next 12 sts, hdc in each of last 8 sts, turn. *(32 hdc, 16 chs)*

Row 4: Ch 1, hdc in each of first 8 sts, sc in each of next 8 chs, hdc in each of next 16 sts, sc in each of next 8 chs, hdc in each of last 8 sts, turn. *(48 sts)*

Row 5: Ch 1, hdc in each of first 8 sts, sc in each of next 8 sts, hdc in each of next 16 sts, sc in each of next 8 sts, hdc in each of last 8 sts, turn.

Rows 6–8: Ch 1, sc in each st across, turn. **Do not turn** at end of last row. *(48 sc)*

Rnd 9: Now working in rnds, ch 1, sc in each st around, **join** *(see Pattern Note)* in beg sc.

Rnd 10: Ch 1, sc in each st around, join in beg sc.

Rnd 11: Ch 1, sc in each of first 10 sts, **sc dec** (*see Stitch Guide*) in next 2 sts, [sc in each of next 10 sts, sc dec in next 2 sts] around, join in beg sc. (*44 sc*)

Rnds 12–14: Ch 1, sc in each st around, join in beg sc.

Rnd 15: Ch 1, sc in each of first 9 sts, sc dec in next 2 sts, [sc in each of next 9 sts, sc dec in next 2 sts] around, join in beg sc. (*40 sc*)

Rnd 16: Ch 1, sc in each st around, join in beg sc.

FIRST LEG
Rnd 1: Ch 1, sc in each of first 2 sts, ch 4, sk next 20 sts, sc in each of last 18 sts, join in beg sc. (*20 sc, 1 ch-4 sp*)

Rnd 2: Ch 1, sc in each st and in each ch around, join in beg sc. (*24 sc*)

Rnds 3–9: Ch 1, sc in each st around, join in beg sc.

Rnd 10: Ch 1, sc in first st, sc dec in next 2 sts, [sc in next st, sc dec in next 2 sts] around, join in beg sc. Fasten off.

2ND LEG
Rnd 1: Join with sc in next skipped st on row 16 of Suit, sc in each st and in each ch on opposite side of ch-4 around, join in beg sc. (*24 sc*)

Rnds 2–10: Rep rnds 2–10 of First Leg.

SLEEVES
Rnd 1: Join copper mist with sc at base of 1 armhole, evenly sp 21 sc around, join in beg sc. (*22 sc*)

Rnd 2: Ch 1, sc in each of first 11 sts, sk next st, sc dec in next 2 sts, sc in each of next 5 sts, sc dec in next 2 sts, sc in last st, join in beg sc. (*19 sc*)

Rnds 3–11: Ch 1, sc in each st around, join in beg sc. Fasten off at end of last rnd.

Rep on other armhole.

Sew snap to top neck opening.

FOOT
MAKE 2.
Rnd 1: With cream, ch 8, 2 sc in 2nd ch from hook, sc in each of next 4 chs, hdc in next ch, 4 hdc in last ch, working on opposite side of ch, hdc in next ch, sc in each of next 4 chs, 2 sc in last ch, join in beg sc. (*18 sts*)

Rnd 2: Ch 1, 2 sc in first st, sc in each of next 5 sts, hdc in next st, 2 hdc in each of next 4 sts, hdc in next st, sc in each of next 5 sts, 2 sc in last st, join in beg sc. Fasten off. (*24 sts*)

Rnd 3: Working this rnd in **back lps** (*see Stitch Guide*), join copper mist with sc in first st, sc in each st around, join in beg sc. (*24 sc*)

Rnd 4: Ch 1, sc in each st around, join in beg sc.

Rnd 5: Ch 1, sc in each of first 8 sts, [**hdc dec** *(see Stitch Guide)* in next 2 sts] 4 times, sc in each of last 8 sts, join in beg sc. *(20 sts)*

Rnd 6: Ch 1, sc in each of first 6 sts, [hdc dec in next 2 sts] 4 times sc in each of last 6 sts, join in beg sc. *(16 sts)*

Rnd 7: Ch 1, sc in each st around, join in beg sc. Fasten off.

With Suit opening at front and toes pointing forward, easing to fit, sew Foot opening to last row of 1 Leg. Rep with other Foot on other Leg.

HOOD
Row 1: With copper mist, ch 13, sc in 2nd ch from hook and in each ch across, turn. *(12 sc)*

Row 2: Ch 1, 2 sc in first st, sc in each st across with 2 sc in last st, turn. *(14 sc)*

Rows 3–5: Ch 1, sc in each st across, turn.

Rows 6 & 7: Ch 1, 2 sc in first st, sc in each st across with 2 sc in last st, turn. *(18 sc at end of last row)*

Rows 8–10: Ch 1, sc in each st across, turn.

Rows 11 & 12: Ch 1, **sc dec** *(see Stitch Guide)* in first 2 sts, sc in each st across to last 2 sts, sc dec in last 2 sts, turn. *(14 sc at end of last row)*

Row 13: Ch 1, sc in each st across. Fasten off.

SIDES
Row 1: Join copper mist with sc in end of row 1 on Hood, sc in end of each of next 12 rows, sc in each st across last row, sc in each of next 13 rows, turn. *(40 sc)*

Rows 2–4: Ch 1, sc in each st across, turn.

Rows 5–7: Ch 1, sc in each of first 12 sts, hdc in each of next 16 sts, sc in each of last 12 sts, turn. *(40 sts)*

Row 8: Ch 1, sc dec first 2 sts, sc in each st across to last 2 sts, sc dec in last 2 sts, turn. *(38 sc)*

Rnd 9: Now working in rnds, ch 1, sc dec in first 2 sts, sc in each of next 10 sts, sc dec in next 2 sts, [sc in each of next 4 sts, sc dec in next 2 sts] twice, sc in each of next 10 sts, sc dec in last 2 sts, working across neck edge, evenly sp 8 sc across ends of rows, working in starting ch on opposite side of row 1, [hdc in next ch, hdc dec in next 2 chs] across, evenly sp 8 sc across ends of rows, join in beg sc. *(57 sts)*

Rnd 10: Ch 1, sc in each of first 41 sts, hdc in each of next 8 sts, sc in each of last 8 sts, join in beg sc. Fasten off.

Leaving first and last 3 sts on neck edge of Suit unsewn, sew neck edge of Hood to neck edge of Suit *(see photo)*.

ANTLER
MAKE 2.
Row 1: With cream, ch 11, sc in 2nd ch from hook and in each of next 8 chs, 4 sc in last ch, working on opposite side of ch, sc in each of next 9 chs, turn. *(22 sc)*

Row 2: Ch 1, sl st in each of first 3 sts, (hdc, dc) in next st, (dc, ch 2, sl st) in next st, sl st in each of next 2 sts, (hdc, tr) in next st, (tr, ch 3, sl st) in next st, sl st in next st, (hdc, dc, tr) in next st, (tr, dc, ch 2, sl st) in next st, sl st in next st, (hdc, tr) in next st, (tr, ch 3, sl st) in next st, sl st in each of next 2 sts, (hdc, dc) in next st, (dc, ch 2, sl st) in next st, sl st in each of last 3 sts. Fasten off.

Sew Antlers to top of head ½ inch apart. ∎

Snowman

SKILL LEVEL

EASY

FINISHED SIZE

Fits 5-inch doll

MATERIALS

- Aunt Lydia's Classic Crochet size 10 crochet cotton (white: 400 yds per ball; solids: 350 yds per ball):
  1 ball each #1 white, #12 black and #494 victory red

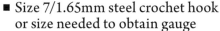

- Size 7/1.65mm steel crochet hook or size needed to obtain gauge
- Sewing needle
- 9mm buttons: 3 black
- 5mm snap: 1
- White sewing thread
- Stitch marker

GAUGE

9 sc = 1 inch

PATTERN NOTE

Join with slip stitch as indicated unless otherwise stated.

INSTRUCTIONS
SUIT

Row 1: Starting at **neck**, with white, ch 29, 2 sc in 2nd ch from hook and in each ch across, turn. *(56 sc)*

Row 2: Ch 1, sc in each st across, turn.

Row 3: Ch 1, hdc in each of first 8 sts, for **armhole**, ch 8, sk next 12 sts, hdc in each of next 16 sts, for **armhole**, ch 8, sk next 12 sts, hdc in each of last 8 sts, turn. *(32 hdc, 16 chs)*

Row 4: Ch 1, hdc in each of first 8 sts, sc in each of next 8 chs, hdc in each of next 16 sts, sc in each of next 8 chs, hdc in each of last 8 sts, turn. *(48 sts)*

Row 5: Ch 1, hdc in each of first 8 sts, sc in each of next 8 sts, hdc in each of next 16 sts, sc in each of next 8 sts, hdc in each of last 8 sts, turn.

Rows 6–9: Ch 1, sc in each st across, turn. **Do not turn** at end of last row. *(48 sc)*

Rnd 10: Now working in rnds, ch 1, sc in each st around, **join** *(see Pattern Note)* in beg sc.

Rnd 11: Ch 1, sc in each of first 10 sts, **sc dec** *(see Stitch Guide)* in next 2 sts, [sc in each of next 10 sts, sc dec in next 2 sts] around, join in beg sc. *(44 sc)*

Rnds 12–14: Ch 1, sc in each st around, join in beg sc.

Rnd 15: Ch 1, sc in each of first 9 sts, sc dec in next 2 sts, [sc in each of next 9 sts, sc dec in next 2 sts] around, join in beg sc. *(40 sc)*

Rnd 16: Ch 1, sc in each st around, join in beg sc.

FIRST LEG
Rnd 1: Ch 1, sc in each of first 2 sts, ch 4, sk next 20 sts, sc in each of last 18 sts, join in beg sc. *(20 sc, 1 ch-4 sp)*

Rnd 2: Ch 1, sc in each st and in each ch around, join in beg sc. *(24 sc)*

Rnds 3–9: Ch 1, sc in each st around, join in beg sc.

Rnd 10: Ch 1, sc in first st, sc dec in next 2 sts, [sc in next st, sc dec in next 2 sts] around, join in beg sc. Fasten off.

2ND LEG
Rnd 1: Join with sc in next sk st on rnd 16 of Suit, sc in each st and in each ch on opposite side of ch-4 around, join in beg sc. *(24 sc)*

Rnds 2–10: Rep rnds 2–10 of First Leg.

SLEEVES
Rnd 1: Join white with sc at base of 1 armhole, evenly sp 21 sc around, join in beg sc. *(22 sc)*

Rnd 2: Ch 1, sc in each of first 11 sts, sk next st, **sc dec** *(see Stitch Guide)* in next 2 sts, sc in each of next 5 sts, sc dec in next 2 sts, sc in last st, join in beg sc. *(19 sc)*

Rnds 3–11: Ch 1, sc in each st around, join in beg sc. Fasten off at end of last rnd.

Rep on other armhole.

Sew buttons evenly sp down front of Suit.

Sew snap to top back opening.

FOOT
MAKE 2.
Rnd 1: With white, ch 8, 2 sc in 2nd ch from hook, sc in each of next 4 chs, hdc in next ch, 4 hdc in last ch, working on opposite side of ch, hdc in next ch, sc in each of next 4 chs, 2 sc in last ch, join in beg sc. *(18 sts)*

Rnd 2: Ch 1, 2 sc in first st, sc in each of next 5 sts, hdc in next st, 2 hdc in each of next 4 sts, hdc in next st, sc in each of next 5 sts, 2 sc in last st, join in beg sc. *(24 sts)*

Rnd 3: Working this rnd in **back lps** *(see Stitch Guide)*, ch 1, sc in each st around, join in beg sc. *(24 sc)*

Rnd 4: Ch 1, sc in each st around, join in beg sc.

Rnd 5: Ch 1, sc in each of first 8 sts, [**hdc dec** *(see Stitch Guide)* in next 2 sts] 4 times, sc in each of last 8 sts, join in beg sc. *(20 sts)*

Rnd 6: Ch 1, sc in each of first 6 sts, [sc dec in next 2 sts] 4 times sc in each of last 6 sts, join in beg sc. *(16 sc)*

Rnd 7: Ch 1, sc in each st around, join in beg sc. Fasten off.

Sew Foot opening to last row of 1 Leg. Rep with other Foot on other Leg.

HAT
Rnd 1: Starting at top, with black, ch 2, 6 sc in 2nd ch from hook, **do not join.** (6 sc)

Note: Do not join or turn rem rnds unless otherwise stated. Mark first st of each rnd.

Rnd 2: 2 sc in each st around. *(12 sc)*

Rnd 3: [Sc in next st, 2 sc in next st] around. *(18 sc)*

Rnd 4: [Sc in each of next 2 sts, 2 sc in next st] around. *(24 sc)*

Rnd 5: [2 sc in next st, sc in each of next 3 sts] around. *(30 sc)*

Row 6: [Sc in each of next 5 sts, 2 sc in next st] around. *(35 sc)*

Rnd 7: [Sc in each of next 4 sts, 2 sc in next st] around. *(42 sc)*

Rnds 8–13: Sc in each st around.

Rnd 14: [Sc in each of next 12 sts, sc dec in next 2 sts] around. *(39 sc)*

Rnd 15: Sc in each st around, join in beg sc, fasten off.

Rnd 16: Join victory red with sc in first st, sc in each st around, join in beg sc.

Rnd 17: Ch 1, sc in each st around, join in beg sc, fasten off.

Rnd 18: Join black with sc in first st, sc in each st around, join in beg sc.

Rnd 19: Ch 1, sc in each of first 2 sts, 2 sc in next st, [sc in each of next 2 sts, 2 sc in next st] around, join in beg sc. *(52 sc)*

Rnd 20: Ch 1, sc in each of first 3 sts, 2 sc in next st, [sc in each of next 3 sts, 2 sc in next st] around, join in beg sc. *(65 sc)*

Rnd 21: Ch 1, sc in each st around, join in beg sc, fasten off.

SCARF

Row 1: With victory red, ch 4, sc in 2nd ch from hook and in each ch across, turn. *(3 sc)*

Rows 2–65: Ch 1, sc in each st across, turn. Fasten off at end of last row.

FRINGE

For each Fringe, cut 2 strands victory red, each 4 inches long. With both strands held tog, fold in half, insert hook in st, pull fold through, pull all loose ends through fold; tighten. Trim ends even.

Attach 1 strand to every st on each short end of Scarf.

MITTEN
MAKE 2.

Rnd 1: With victory red, ch 2, 6 sc in 2nd ch from hook, **do not join.** *(6 sc)*

Rnd 2: 2 sc in each st around. *(12 sc)*

Rnd 3: [Sc in each of next 2 sts, 2 sc in next st] around. *(16 sc)*

Rnd 4: [Sc in each of next 7 sts, 2 sc in next st] around. *(18 sc)*

Rnd 5: Sc in each st around.

Rnd 6: For **thumb**, ch 4, 2 hdc in 3rd ch from hook, hdc in next ch, sc in each of next 18 sts. *(18 sc, 3 hdc)*

Rnd 7: Sk thumb, [sc in each of next 7 sts, sc dec in next 2 sts] around. *(16 sc)*

Rnd 8: [Sc in each of next 6 sts, sc dec in next 2 sts] around. *(14 sc)*

Rnd 9: Sc in each st around.

Rnd 10: Sc in each st around, join in beg sc, fasten off. ■

We wish you a
Merry Christmas!

Create a family tradition and decorate
year after year with these little cuties!

Pilgrim Girl

SKILL LEVEL

EASY

FINISHED SIZE
Fits 5-inch doll

MATERIALS
- Aunt Lydia's Classic Crochet size 10 crochet cotton (white: 400 yds per ball; solids: 350 yds per ball):
    1 ball each #1 white and #12 black
- Size 7/1.65mm steel crochet hook or size needed to obtain gauge
- 5mm snap: 1
- Sewing needle
- White sewing thread

GAUGE
9 sc = 1 inch

PATTERN NOTES
Join with slip stitch as indicated unless otherwise stated.

Chain-3 at beginning of round or row counts as first double crochet unless otherwise stated.

Chain-2 at beginning of round or row counts as first half double crochet unless otherwise stated.

INSTRUCTIONS
DRESS
Row 1: Starting at **neck**, with black, ch 29, 2 sc in 2nd ch from hook and in each ch across, turn. *(56 sc)*

Row 2: Ch 1, sc in each st across, turn.

Row 3: Ch 1, hdc in each of first 8 sts, for **armhole**, ch 8, sk next 12 sts, hdc in each of next 16 sts, for **armhole**, ch 8, sk next 12 sts, hdc in each of last 8 sts, turn. *(32 hdc, 16 chs)*

Row 4: Ch 1, hdc in each of first 8 sts, sc in each of next 8 chs, hdc in each of next 16 sts, sc in each of next 8 chs, hdc in each of last 8 sts, turn. *(48 sts)*

Row 5: Ch 1, hdc in each of first 8 sts, sc in each of next 8 sts, hdc in each of next 16 sts, sc in each of next 8 sts, hdc in each of last 8 sts, turn.

Rnd 6: Now working in rnds, ch 1, sc in each st around, **join** *(see Pattern Notes)* in beg sc.

Rnd 7: For **skirt, ch 3** *(see Pattern Notes)*, 2 dc in next st, [dc in next st, 2 dc in next st] around, join in 3rd ch of beg ch-3. *(72 dc)*

Rnds 8–14: Ch 3, dc in each st around, join in 3rd ch of beg ch-3.

Rnd 15: Ch 1, [sl st in next st, ch 1] around, join in joining sl st of last rnd.

COLLAR
Row 1: With RS facing, working in starting ch on opposite side of row 1, join white with sc in first ch, sc in same st, sc in each ch across with 2 sc in last ch, turn. *(30 sc)*

Row 2: Working this row in **front lps** *(see Stitch Guide)*, **ch 2** *(see Pattern Notes)*, hdc in same st, 2 hdc in each st across, turn. *(60 hdc)*

Row 3: Ch 2, hdc in each of next 3 sts, 2 hdc in next st, [hdc in each of next 4 sts, 2 hdc in next st] across, turn. *(72 hdc)*

Row 4: Ch 1, sc in each st across. Fasten off.

SLEEVES
Rnd 1: Join black with sc at base of 1 armhole, evenly sp 21 sc around, join with in beg sc. *(22 sc)*

Rnd 2: Ch 1, sc in each of first 12 sts, **sc dec** *(see Stitch Guide)* in next 2 sts, sc in each of next 5 sts, sc dec in next 2 sts, sc in last st, join in beg sc. *(20 sc)*

Rnds 3–10: Ch 1, sc in each st around, join in beg sc. Fasten off at end of last rnd.

Rnd 11: For **cuff**, join white with sc in first st, sc in each st around, join in beg sc.

Rnd 12: Working this rnd in **back lps** *(see Stitch Guide)*, sc in each of first 9 sts, 2 sc in next st, sc in each of next 9 sts, 2 sc in last st, join in beg sc. *(22 sc)*

Rnd 13: Ch 1, sc in each of first 10 sts, 2 sc in next st, sc in each of next 10 sts, 2 sc in next st, join in beg sc. *(24 sc)*

Rnd 14: Ch 1, [sl st in next st, ch 1] around, join in joining sl st of last rnd. Fasten off.

Turn cuffs up.

Rep on other armhole.

Sew snap to top back opening of Dress.

APRON
Row 1: Starting at **waist**, ch 15, sc in 2nd ch from hook and in each ch across, turn. *(14 sc)*

Row 2: Ch 3, 2 dc in next st, [dc in next st, 2 dc in next st] across, turn. *(21 dc)*

Rows 3–7: Ch 3, dc in each st across, turn. Fasten off at end of last row.

For **ties**, join white in end of row 1, ch 45. Fasten off. Rep at opposite end of row 1.

BLOOMERS
Rnd 1: With white, ch 38, join in beg ch to form ring, ch 1, sc in first ch and in each ch around, join in beg sc. *(38 sc)*

Rnds 2–9: Ch 1, sc in each st around, join in beg sc.

FIRST LEG
Rnd 1: Ch 5, sk first 19 sts, sc in each of next 19 sts, sc in each of first 5 chs, join in beg sc. *(24 sc)*

Rnds 2–9: Ch 1, sc in each st around, join in beg sc.

Rnd 10: Ch 1, sc in first st, ch 2, [sc in next st, ch 2] around, join in beg sc. Fasten off.

2ND LEG
Rnd 1: Working on opposite side of ch-5, join white with sc in first ch, sc in each of next 4 chs, sc in each of next 19 sk sts on rnd 9 of Bloomers, join in beg sc. *(24 sc)*

Rnds 2–10: Rep rnds 2–10 of First Leg.

SHOE
MAKE 2.

Rnd 1: With black, ch 8, 2 sc in 2nd ch from hook, sc in each of next 4 chs, hdc in next ch, 4 hdc in last ch, working on opposite side of ch, hdc in next ch, sc in each of next 4 chs, 2 sc in last ch, join in beg sc. *(18 sts)*

Rnd 2: Ch 1, 2 sc in first st, sc in each of next 5 sts, hdc in next st, 2 hdc in each of next 4 sts, hdc in next st, sc in each of next 5 sts, 2 sc in last st, join in beg sc. *(24 sts)*

Rnd 3: Working this rnd in back lps, ch 1, sc in each st around, join in beg sc. *(24 sc)*

Rnd 4: Ch 1, sc in each st around, join in beg sc.

Rnd 5: Ch 1, sc in each of first 8 sts, [**hdc dec** *(see Stitch Guide)* in next 2 sts] 4 times, sc in each of last 8 sts, join in beg sc. *(20 sts)*

Rnd 6: Ch 1, sc in each of first 9 sts, sc dec in next 2 sts, sc in each of last 9 sts, join in beg sc. *(19 sc)*

Rnd 7: Ch 1, sc in each of first 7 sts, [sc dec in next 2 sts] 3 times, sc in each of last 6 sts, join in beg sc. Fasten off.

HAT

Rnd 1: With white, ch 4, join in beg ch to form ring, ch 3, 11 dc in ring, join in 3rd ch of beg ch-3. *(12 dc)*

Rnd 2: Ch 3, dc in same st, 2 dc in each st around, join in 3rd ch of beg ch-3. *(24 dc)*

Rnd 3: Ch 3, 2 dc in next st, [dc in next st, 2 dc in next st] around, join in 3rd ch of beg ch-3. *(36 dc)*

Rnd 4: Ch 3, dc in next st, 2 dc in next st, [dc in each of next 2 sts, 2 dc in next st] around, join in 3rd ch of beg ch-3. *(48 dc)*

Rnd 5: Ch 3, dc in each of next 4 sts, 2 dc in next st, [dc in each of next 5 sts, 2 dc in next st] around, join in 3rd ch of beg ch-3. *(56 dc)*

Rnd 6: Ch 3, dc in each st around, join in 3rd ch of beg ch-3.

Rnd 7: Ch 1, sc in first st, sc dec in next 2 sts, [sc in next st, sc dec in next 2 sts] around to last 2 sts, sc dec in last 2 sts, join in beg sc. *(37 sc)*

Row 8: Now working in rows, for **brim**, ch 1, sc in each of first 27 sts, leaving rem sts unworked, turn. *(27 sc)*

Rows 9–12: Ch 1, sc in each st across, turn. Fasten off at end of last row. ■

Pilgrim Boy

SKILL LEVEL

EASY

FINISHED SIZE
Fits 5-inch doll

MATERIALS
- Aunt Lydia's Classic Crochet size 10 crochet cotton (white: 400 yds per ball; solids: 350 yds per ball):
    1 ball each #1 white and #12 black
- Size 7/1.65mm steel crochet hook or size needed to obtain gauge
- Sewing needle
- Embroidery needle
- Gold 6-strand embroidery floss
- 9mm buttons: 2 black
- Black sewing thread
- Stitch marker

GAUGE
9 sc = 1 inch

PATTERN NOTE
Join with slip stitch as indicated unless otherwise stated.

INSTRUCTIONS
JACKET
Row 1: Starting at **neck**, with black, ch 29, 2 sc in 2nd ch from hook and in each ch across, turn. (56 sc)

Row 2: Ch 1, sc in first st, for **buttonhole**, ch 2, sk next 2 sts, sc in each st across, turn. (54 sc, 1 ch-2 sp)

Row 3: Ch 1, hdc in each of first 8 sts, for **armhole**, ch 8, sk next 12 sts, hdc in each of next 16 sts, for **armhole**, ch 8, sk next 12 sts, hdc in each of next 5 sts, hdc in each of next 2 chs, hdc in last ch, turn. (32 hdc, 16 chs)

Row 4: Ch 1, hdc in each of first 8 sts, sc in each of next 8 chs, hdc in each of next 16 sts, sc in each of next 8 chs, hdc in each of last 8 sts, turn. (48 sts)

Row 5: Ch 1, hdc in each of first 8 sts, sc in each of next 8 sts, hdc in each of next 16 sts, sc in each of next 8 sts, hdc in each of last 8 sts, turn.

Row 6: Rep row 2.

Row 7: Ch 1, sc in each st and each ch across, turn. (48 sc)

Rows 8–13: Ch 1, sc in each st across, turn. Fasten off at end of last row.

SLEEVES

Rnd 1: Join black with sc at base of 1 armhole, evenly sp 21 sc around, **join** (see Pattern Note) in beg sc. (22 sc)

Rnd 2: Ch 1, sc in each of first 11 sts, sk next st, **sc dec** (see Stitch Guide) in next 2 sts, sc in each of next 5 sts, sc dec in next 2 sts, sc in last st, join in beg sc. (19 sc)

Rnds 3–10: Ch 1, sc in each st around, join in beg sc. Fasten off at end of last rnd.

Rnd 11: For **cuff**, join white with sc in first st, sc in each st around, join in beg sc, turn.

Rnd 12: Working this rnd in **back lps** (see Stitch Guide), sc in each of first 9 sts, 2 sc in next st, sc in each of last 9 sts, join in beg sc. (20 sc)

Rnd 13: Ch 1, sc in each of first 4 sts, 2 sc in next st, [sc in each of next 4 sts, 2 sc in next st] around, join in beg sc. (24 sc)

Rep on other armhole.

Turn cuff down.

COLLAR

Row 1: With WS facing, working in starting ch on opposite side of row 1, join white with sc in first ch, sc in same st, sc in each ch across with 2 sc in last ch, turn. (30 sc)

Row 2: Ch 1, 2 hdc in first st, hdc in each of next 4 sts, *3 hdc in next st, hdc in each of next 3 sts, 3 hdc in next st*, hdc in each of next 10 sts, rep between * once, hdc in each of next 4 sts, 2 hdc in last st, turn. (40 hdc)

Row 3: Ch 1, hdc in each of first 7 sts, 3 hdc in next st, hdc in each of next 5 sts, 3 hdc in next st, hdc in each of next 12 sts, 3 hdc in next st, hdc in each of next 5 sts, 3 hdc in next st, hdc in each of least 7 sts, turn. (48 hdc)

Row 4: Ch 1, hdc in each of first 8 sts, 3 hdc in next st, hdc in each of next 7 sts, 3 hdc in next st, hdc in each of next 14 sts, 3 hdc in next st, hdc in each of next 7 sts, 3 hdc in next st, hdc in each of next 8 sts, turn. (56 hdc)

Row 5: Ch 1, sc in each of first 10 sts, fasten off, sk next 36 sts, join with sc in next st, sc in each of last 9 sts. Fasten off.

Sew 2 buttons to left front opposite buttonholes.

BREECHES

Rnd 1: With black, ch 38, join in beg ch to form ring, ch 1, sc in first ch and in each ch around, join in beg sc. (38 sc)

Rnds 2–9: Ch 1, sc in each st around, join in beg sc.

FIRST LEG

Rnd 1: Ch 7, sk first 19 sts, sc in each of next 19 sts, sc in each of first 7 chs, join in beg sc. *(26 sc)*

Rnds 2 & 3: Ch 1, sc in each st around, join in beg sc.

Rnd 4: Ch 1, sc in each of first 4 sts, sc dec in next 2 sts, sc in each of next 5 sts, sc dec in next 2 sts, sc in each of next 4 sts, sc dec in next 2 sts, sc in each of next 5 sts, sc dec in last 2 sts, join in beg sc. *(22 sc)*

Rnd 5: Working this rnd in **front lps** *(see Stitch Guide)*, ch 1, sc in each of first 3 sts, sc dec in next 2 sts, sc in each of next 4 sts, sc dec next 2 sts, sc in each of next 3 sts, sc dec in next 2 sts, sc in each of next 4 sts, sc dec in last 2 sts, join in beg sc. Fasten off.

2ND LEG

Rnd 1: Working on opposite side of ch-7, join black with sc in first ch, sc in each of next 6 chs, sc in each of next 19 skipped sts on rnd 9 of Breeches, join in beg sc. *(26 sc)*

Rnds 2–5: Rep rnds 2–5 of First Leg.

SHOE
MAKE 2.

Rnd 1: With black, ch 8, 2 sc in 2nd ch from hook, sc in each of next 4 chs, hdc in next ch, 4 hdc in last ch, working on opposite side of ch, hdc in next ch, sc in each of next 4 chs, 2 sc in last ch, join in beg sc. *(18 sts)*

Rnd 2: Ch 1, 2 sc in first st, sc in each of next 5 sts, hdc in next st, 2 hdc in each of next 4 sts, hdc in next st, sc in each of next 5 sts, 2 sc in last st, join in beg sc. *(24 sts)*

Rnd 3: Working this rnd in back lps, ch 1, sc in each st around, join in beg sc. *(24 sc)*

Rnd 4: Ch 1, sc in each st around, join in beg sc.

Rnd 5: Ch 1, sc in each of first 8 sts, [**hdc dec** *(see Stitch Guide)* in next 2 sts] 4 times, sc in each of last 8 sts, join in beg sc. *(20 sts)*

Rnd 6: Ch 1, sc in each of first 9 sts, sc dec in next 2 sts, sc in each of last 9 sts, join in beg sc. Fasten off. *(19 sc)*

Rnd 7: Working this rnd in back lps, for **sock**, join white with sc in first st, sc in each of next 6 sts, [sc dec in next 2 sts] 3 times, sc in each of last 6 sts, join in beg sc. *(16 sc)*

Rnds 8–11: Ch 1, sc in each st around, join in beg sc.

Rnd 12: Ch 1, sc in each of first 7 sts, 2 sc in next st, sc in each of next 7 sts, 2 sc in next st, join in beg sc. Fasten off.

With gold floss, using **straight stitch** *(see Fig. 1)*, embroider a square on toe of Shoe for buckle.

Fig. 1
Straight Stitch

Sew Last rnd of Shoe to last rnd of 1 Leg on Breeches. Rep with other Shoe on other Leg.

HAT

Rnd 1: With black, ch 2, 7 sc in 2nd ch from hook, **do not join**. *(7 sc)*

Note: Do not join or turn rem rnds unless otherwise stated. Mark first st of each rnd.

Rnd 2: 2 sc in each st around. *(14 sc)*

Rnd 3: [Sc in next st, 2 sc in next st] around. *(21 sc)*

Rnd 4: Working this rnd in back lps, sc in each st around.

Rnd 5: Sc in each st around.

Rnd 6: [Sc in each of next 6 sts, 2 sc in next st] around. *(24 sc)*

Rnd 7: Sc in each st around.

Rnd 8: [Sc in each of next 7 sts, 2 sc in next st] around. *(27 sc)*

Rnd 9: Sc in each st around.

Rnd 10: [Sc in each of next 8 sts, 2 sc in next st] around. *(30 sc)*

Rnd 11: Sc in each st around.

Rnd 12: [Sc in each of next 9 sts, 2 sc in next st] around. *(33 sc)*

Rnd 13: [Sc in each of next 10 sts, 2 sc in next st] around. *(36 sc)*

Rnd 14: [Sc in each of next 8 sts, 2 sc in next st] around. *(40 sc)*

Rnd 15: [2 sc in next st, sc in each of next 7 sts] around, join in beg sc. *(45 sc)*

Rnd 16: Working this rnd in front lps, ch 1, hdc in each of first 2 sts, 2 hdc in next st, [hdc in each of next 2 sts, 2 hdc in next st] around, join in top of beg hdc. *(60 hdc)*

Rnd 17: Ch 1, hdc in each of first 4 sts, 2 hdc in next st, [hdc in each of next 4 sts, 2 hdc in next st] around, join in top of beg hdc. *(72 hdc)*

Rnd 18: Ch 1, sc in each st around, join in beg sc. Fasten off.

BAND
With black, ch 46, sc in 2nd ch from hook and in each ch across. Fasten off.

Sew Band around rnd 15 of Hat; tack ends tog.

For buckle, with gold floss, using straight stitch, embroider a square on Band for center front of Hat. ■

Easter Bunny

SKILL LEVEL

EASY

FINISHED SIZE
Fits 5-inch doll

MATERIALS
- Aunt Lydia's Classic Crochet size 10 crochet cotton (white: 400 yds per ball; solids: 350 yds per ball; multis: 300 yds per ball): 1 ball each #210 antique white, #401 orchid pink, #428 mint green, #465 pastels ombre, #431 pumpkin and #622 kerry green
- Size 7/1.65mm steel crochet hook or size needed to obtain gauge
- Sewing needle
- 5mm snap: 1
- 1-inch white pompom
- Polyester fiberfill
- White sewing thread
- Stitch marker

GAUGE
9 sc = 1 inch

PATTERN NOTE
Join with slip stitch as indicated unless otherwise stated.

INSTRUCTIONS
SUIT
Row 1: Starting at **neck**, with antique white, ch 29, 2 sc in 2nd ch from hook and in each ch across, turn. *(56 sc)*

Row 2: Ch 1, sc in each st across, turn.

Row 3: Ch 1, hdc in each of first 8 sts, for **armhole**, ch 8, sk next 12 sts, hdc in each of next 16 sts, for **armhole**, ch 8, sk next 12 sts, hdc in each of last 8 sts, turn. *(32 hdc, 16 chs)*

Row 4: Ch 1, hdc in each of first 8 sts, sc in each of next 8 chs, hdc in each of next 16 sts, sc in each of next 8 chs, hdc in each of last 8 sts, turn. *(48 sts)*

Row 5: Ch 1, hdc in each of first 8 sts, sc in each of next 8 sts, hdc in each of next 16 sts, sc in each of next 8 sts, hdc in each of last 8 sts, turn.

Rows 6–9: Ch 1, sc in each st across, turn. **Do not turn** at end of last row. *(48 sc)*

Rnd 10: Now working in rnds, ch 1, sc in each st around, **join** *(see Pattern Note)* in beg sc.

Rnd 11: Ch 1, sc in each of first 10 sts, **sc dec** *(see Stitch Guide)* in next 2 sts, [sc in each of next 10 sts, sc dec in next 2 sts] around, join in beg sc. *(44 sc)*

Rnds 12–14: Ch 1, sc in each st around, join in beg sc.

Rnd 15: Ch 1, sc in each of first 9 sts, sc dec in next 2 sts, [sc in each of next 9 sts, sc dec in next 2 sts] around, join in beg sc. *(40 sc)*

Rnd 16: Ch 1, sc in each st around, join in beg sc.

FIRST LEG
Rnd 1: Ch 1, sc in each of first 2 sts, ch 4, sk next 20 sts, sc in each of last 18 sts, join in beg sc. *(20 sc, 1 ch-4 sp)*

Rnd 2: Ch 1, sc in each st and in each ch around, join in beg sc. *(24 sc)*

Rnds 3–9: Ch 1, sc in each st around, join in beg sc.

Rnd 10: Ch 1, sc in first st, sc dec in next 2 sts, [sc in next st, sc dec in next 2 sts] around, join in beg sc. Fasten off.

2ND LEG

Rnd 1: Join with sc in next sk st on row 16 of Suit, sc in each st and in each ch on opposite side of ch-4 around, join in beg sc. *(24 sc)*

Rnds 2–10: Rep rnds 2–10 of First Leg.

SLEEVES

Rnd 1: Join antique white with sc at base of 1 armhole, evenly sp 21 sc around, join with in beg sc. *(22 sc)*

Rnd 2: Ch 1, sc in each of first 11 sts, sk next st, **sc dec** *(see Stitch Guide)* in next 2 sts, sc in each of next 5 sts, sc dec in next 2 sts, sc in last st, join in beg sc. *(19 sc)*

Rnds 3–11: Ch 1, sc in each st around, join in beg sc. Fasten off at end of last rnd.

Rep on other armhole.

FOOT
MAKE 2.

Rnd 1: With orchid pink, ch 8, 2 sc in 2nd ch from hook, sc in each of next 4 chs, hdc in next ch, 4 hdc in last ch, working on opposite side of ch, hdc in next ch, sc in each of next 4 chs, 2 sc in last ch, join in beg sc. Fasten off. *(18 sts)*

Rnd 2: Join antique white with sc in first st, sc in same st, sc in each of next 5 sts, hdc in next st, 2 hdc in each of next 4 sts, hdc in next st, sc in each of next 5 sts, 2 sc in last st, join in beg sc. *(24 sts)*

Rnd 3: Working this rnd in **back lps** *(see Stitch Guide)*, ch 1, sc in each st around, join in beg sc. *(24 sc)*

Rnd 4: Ch 1, sc in each st around, join in beg sc.

Rnd 5: Ch 1, sc in each of first 8 sts, [**hdc dec** *(see Stitch Guide)* in next 2 sts] 4 times, sc in each of last 8 sts, join in beg sc. *(20 sts)*

Rnd 6: Ch 1, sc in each of first 6 sts, [hdc dec in next 2 sts] 4 times sc in each of last 6 sts, join in beg sc. *(16 sts)*

Rnd 7: Ch 1, sc in each st around, join in beg sc. Fasten off.

With Suit opening at front, easing to fit, sew Foot opening to last row of 1 Leg. Rep with other Foot on other Leg.

Sew snap to top neck opening.

HOOD

Row 1: With antique white, ch 13, sc in 2nd ch from hook and in each ch across, turn. *(12 sc)*

Row 2: Ch 1, 2 sc in first st, sc in each st across with 2 sc in last st, turn. *(14 sc)*

Rows 3–5: Ch 1, sc in each st across, turn.

Rows 6 & 7: Ch 1, 2 sc in first st, sc in each st across with 2 sc in last st, turn. *(18 sc at end of last row)*

Rows 8–10: Ch 1, sc in each st across, turn.

Rows 11 & 12: Ch 1, **sc dec** *(see Stitch Guide)* in first 2 sts, sc in each st across to last 2 sts, sc dec in last 2 sts, turn. *(14 sc at end of last row)*

Row 13: Ch 1, sc in each st across. Fasten off.

SIDES

Row 1: Join antique white with sc in end of row 1 on Hood, sc in end of each of next 12 rows, sc in each st across last row, sc in each of next 13 rows, turn. *(40 sc)*

Rows 2–4: Ch 1, sc in each st across, turn.

Rows 5–7: Ch 1, sc in each of first 12 sts, hdc in each of next 16 sts, sc in each of last 12 sts, turn. *(40 sts)*

Row 8: Ch 1, sc dec in first 2 sts, sc in each st across to last 2 sts, sc dec in last 2 sts, turn. *(38 sc)*

Rnd 9: Now working in rnds, ch 1, sc dec in first 2 sts, sc in each of next 10 sts, sc dec in next 2 sts, [sc in each of next 4 sts, sc dec in next 2 sts] twice, sc in each of next 10 sts, sc dec in last 2 sts, working across neck edge, evenly sp 8 sc across ends of rows, working in starting ch on opposite side of row 1, [hdc in next ch, hdc dec in next 2 chs] across, evenly sp 8 sc across ends of rows, join in beg sc. *(57 sts)*

Rnd 10: Ch 1, sc in each of first 41 sts, hdc in each of next 8 sts, sc in each of last 8 sts, join in beg sc. Fasten off.

Leaving first and last 3 sts on neck edge of Suit unsewn, sew neck edge of Hood to neck edge of Suit.

EAR
MAKE 2.
INNER EAR

Row 1: With orchid pink, ch 11, sc in 2nd ch from hook and in each of next 4 chs, hdc in each of next 2 chs, dc in each of next 2 chs, 6 dc in last ch, working on opposite side of starting ch, dc in each of next 2 chs, hdc in each of next 2 chs, sc in each of last 5 chs, turn. *(24 sts)*

Row 2: Ch 1, sc in each of first 11 sts, 2 sc in each of next 2 sts, sc in each of last 11 sts. Fasten off. *(26 sc)*

OUTER EAR

Rows 1 & 2: With antique white, rep rows 1 and 2 of Inner Ear. **Do not fasten off** at end of last row.

Row 3: Holding WS of Inner Ear to RS of Outer Ear with Inner Ear facing, matching sts, working through both thicknesses, ch 1, sc in each of first 12 sts, 2 sc in each of next 2 sts, sc in each of last 12 sts. Fasten off.

Sew Ears to top of Hood ¾ inch apart.

Sew pompom to back of Suit for tail.

BASKET

Rnd 1: With mint green, ch 2, 6 sc in 2nd ch from hook, **do not join**. *(6 sc)*

Note: Do not join or turn rem rnds unless otherwise stated. Mark first st of each rnd.

Rnd 2: 2 sc in each st around. *(12 sc)*

Rnd 3: [Sc in next st, 2 sc in next st] around. *(18 sc)*

Rnd 4: [Sc in each of next 6 sts, 2 sc in each of next 3 sts] twice. *(24 sc)*

Rnd 5: *Sc in each of next 6 sts, [2 sc in next st, sc in next st] 3 times, rep from *. *(30 sc)*

Rnd 6: Sc in each of first 8 sts, [2 sc in next st, sc in next st] 3 times, sc in each of next 9 sts, [2 sc in next st, sc in next st] 3 times, sc in last st, join in beg sc. *(36 sc)*

Rnd 7: Working this rnd in back lps, ch 1, sc in each st around, join in beg sc.

Rnd 8: Ch 1, sc in each st around, join in beg sc.

Rnd 9: Ch 1, sc in each of first 7 sts, sc dec in next 2 sts, [sc in each of next 7 sts, sc dec in next 2 sts] around, join in beg sc. *(32 sc)*

Rnds 10–13: Ch 1, sc in each st around, join in beg sc. Fasten off.

Rnd 14: Join pastels ombre in any st, ch 2, dc in same st, sk next st, *[sl st, ch 2, dc] in next st, sk next st, rep from * around, join in joining sl st. Fasten off.

HANDLE

With pastels ombre, ch 21, sc in 2nd ch from hook and in each ch across. Fasten off.

Sew Handle ends to each side of Basket on inside.

CARROT
MAKE 2.

Rnd 1: With pumpkin, ch 2, 6 sc in 2nd ch from hook, **do not join**. *(6 sc)*

Rnd 2: [Sc in next st, 2 sc in next st] around. *(9 sc)*

Rnds 3 & 4: Sc in each st around.

Rnd 5: Sc in each of first 4 sts, 2 sc in next st, sc in each of last 4 sts. *(10 sc)*

Rnd 6: Sc in each st around.

Rnd 7: Sc in each st around with 2 sc in last st. *(11 sc)*

Rnd 8: Sc in each st around.

Rnd 9: Sc in each of first 5 sts, 2 sc in next st, sc in each of last 5 sts. *(12 sc)*

Rnds 10–11: Sc in each st around. Fasten off at end of last rnd. Stuff.

Rnd 12: Working this rnd in back lps, join kerry green in first st, ch 1, sc dec in first 2 sts, [sc dec in next 2 sts] around, join in beg sc. Fasten off.

CARROT TOP
For each Carrot Top, cut 2 strands kerry green, each 4 inches long. With both strands held tog, fold in half, insert hook in st, pull fold through, pull all loose ends through fold, tighten. Trim ends.

Attach 1 Carrot Top to each st of rnd 12. ■

Uncle Sam

SKILL LEVEL

EASY

FINISHED SIZE
Fits 5-inch doll

MATERIALS
- Aunt Lydia's Classic Crochet size 10 crochet cotton (white: 400 yds per ball; solids: 350 yds per ball):
  1 ball each #494 victory red, #1 white, #12 black, #487 dark royal
- Size 7/1.65mm steel crochet hook or size needed to obtain gauge
- Tapestry needle
- Sewing needle
- 8mm buttons: 3 white
- Blue and white sewing thread
- Stitch marker

GAUGE
9 sc = 1 inch

PATTERN NOTE
Join with slip stitch as indicated unless otherwise stated.

INSTRUCTIONS
COAT
Row 1: Starting at **neck**, with dark royal, ch 29, 2 sc in 2nd ch from hook and in each ch across, turn. *(56 sc)*

Row 2: Ch 1, sc in first st, for **buttonhole**, ch 2, sk next 2 sts, sc in each st across, turn. *(54 sc, 1 ch-2 sp)*

Row 3: Ch 1, hdc in each of first 8 sts, for **armhole**, ch 8, sk next 12 sts, hdc in each of next 16 sts, for **armhole**, ch 8, sk next 12 sts, hdc in each of last 8 sts, turn. *(32 hdc, 16 chs)*

Row 4: Ch 1, hdc in each of first 8 sts, sc in each of next 8 chs, hdc in each of next 16 sts, sc in each of next 8 chs, hdc in each of next 5 sts, 2 hdc in next ch sp, hdc in last st, turn. *(48 sts)*

Row 5: Ch 1, hdc in each of first 8 sts, sc in each of next 8 sts, hdc in each of next 16 sts, sc in each of next 8 sts, hdc in each of last 8 sts, turn.

Row 6: Rep row 2.

Row 7: Ch 1, sc in each st across with 2 sc in ch-2 sp, turn

Rows 8 & 9: Ch 1, sc in each st across, turn.

RIGHT FRONT
Row 1: Ch 1, sc in first st, for **buttonhole**, ch 2, sk next 2 sts, sc in each of next 9 sts, sl st in next st, leaving rem sts unworked, turn. *(10 sc, 1 ch-2 sp, 1 sl st)*

Row 2: Sk first sl st, sc in each of next 4 sts, hdc in each of next 4 sts, sc in next st, 2 sc in next ch sp, sc in last st, turn. *(12 sts)*

Row 3: Ch 1, sc in each of first 4 sts, hdc in each of next 4 sts, sc in each of last 4 sts, turn.

Row 4: Ch 1, sc in each of first 4 sts, hdc in next st, 2 dc in each of next 2 sts, hdc in next st, sc in each of next 2 sts, sl st in each of last 2 sts. Fasten off.

FIRST TAIL
Row 1: Sk next 3 unworked sts on row 9 of Coat, join with sc in next st, sc in each of next 6 sts, leaving rem sts unworked, turn. *(7 sc)*

Rows 2 & 3: Ch 1, sc in each st across, turn.

Row 4: Ch 1, **sc dec** *(see Stitch Guide)* in first 2 sts, sc in each of next 3 sts, sc dec in last 2 sts, turn. *(5 sc)*

Row 5: Ch 1, sc in each st across, turn.

Row 6: Ch 1, sc dec in first 2 sts, sc in next st, sc dec in last 2 sts, turn. *(3 sc)*

Row 7: Ch 1, sc in each st across, turn.

Row 8: Ch 1, sc dec in first 2 sts, sl st in last st. Fasten off.

Sk next 2 sts on row 9 of Coat and rep First Tail.

LEFT FRONT
Row 1: Sk next 3 unworked sts on row 9 of Coat, join with sc in next st, sc in each of last 12 sts, turn. *(13 sts)*

Row 2: Ch 1, sc in each of first 4 sts, hdc in each of next 4 sts, sc in each of next 4 sts, leaving rem st unworked, turn.

Row 3: Ch 1, sc in each of first 4 sts, hdc in each of next 4 sts, sc in each of last 4 sts, turn.

Row 4: Sl st in each of first 2 sts, sc in each of next 2 sts, hdc in next st, 2 dc in each of next 2 sts, hdc in next st, sc in each of last 4 sts. Fasten off.

NECK TRIM
Working in starting ch on opposite side of Coat, join white with sc in first ch, sc in same ch, sc in each ch across with 2 sc in last ch. Fasten off.

SLEEVES
Rnd 1: Join dark royal with sc at base of 1 armhole, evenly sp 21 sc around, **join** *(see Pattern Notes)* in beg sc. *(22 sc)*

Rnd 2: Ch 1, sc in each of first 12 sts, **sc dec** *(see Stitch Guide)* in next 2 sts, sc in each of next 5 sts, sc dec in next 2 sts, sc in last st, join in beg sc. *(20 sc)*

Rnds 3–4: Ch 1, sc in each st around, join in beg sc.

Rnd 5: Ch 1, sc in each of first 8 sts, sc dec in next 2 sts, sc in each of next 8 sts, sc dec in last 2 sts, join in beg sc. *(18 sc)*

Rnds 6–11: Ch 1, sc in each st around, join in beg sc. Fasten off at end of last rnd.

Rep on other armhole.

Sew buttons down Left Front opposite buttonholes.

PANTS SIDE
MAKE 2.
Row 1: With victory red, ch 20, sc in 2nd ch from hook and in each ch across, **changing color** *(see Stitch Guide)* to white in last st, turn. *(19 sc)*

Row 2: Ch 1, sc in each st across, turn.

Row 3: Ch 1, sc in each st across, changing to victory red in last st, turn.

Row 4: Ch 1, sc in each st across, turn.

Row 5: Ch 1, sc in each st across, changing to white in last st, turn.

Rows 6–21: [Rep rows 2–5 consecutively] 4 times.

Rows 22 & 23: Rep rows 2 and 3.

Row 24: Ch 1, sc in each st across. Fasten off.

Sew first 9 sts on first and last rows tog for leg.

For Pants front seam, sew last sts of row 1 on 1 Pants Side to last sts of row 24 on other Pants Side. Rep for back seam.

Turn up bottom of Pants legs up to form cuffs *(see photo)*.

WAISTBAND
Working in ends of rows at waist edge of Pants, join victory red with sc in first row, sc in next row, sc dec in next 2 rows [sc in each of next 2 rows, sc dec in next 2 rows] around, join in beg sc. Fasten off.

SHOE
MAKE 2.
Rnd 1: With black, ch 8, 2 sc in 2nd ch from hook, sc in each of next 4 chs, hdc in next ch, 4 hdc in last ch, working on opposite side of ch, hdc in next ch, sc in each of next 4 chs, 2 sc in last ch, join in beg sc. *(18 sts)*

Rnd 2: Ch 1, 2 sc in first st, sc in each of next 5 sts, hdc in next st, 2 hdc in each of next 4 sts, hdc in next st, sc in each of next 5 sts, 2 sc in last st, join in beg sc. *(24 sts)*

Rnd 3: Working this rnd in **back lps** *(see Stitch Guide)*, ch 1, sc in each st around, join in beg sc. *(24 sc)*

Rnd 4: Ch 1, sc in each st around, join in beg sc.

Rnd 5: Ch 1, sc in each of first 8 sts, [**hdc dec** *(see Stitch Guide)* in next 2 sts] 4 times, sc in each of last 8 sts, join in beg sc. *(20 sts)*

Rnd 6: Ch 1, sc in each of first 9 sts, sc dec in next 2 sts, sc in each of last 9 sts, join in beg sc. *(19 sts)*

Rnd 7: Ch 1, sc in each of first 7 sts, [sc dec in next 2 sts] 3 times, sc in each of last 6 sts, join in beg sc. Fasten off. *(16 sc)*

HAT
SIDES
Row 1: With victory red, ch 9, sc in 2nd ch from hook and in each ch across, turn. *(8 sc)*

Row 2: Ch 1, sc in each st across, changing to white in last st, turn.

Row 3: Ch 1, sc in each st across, turn.

Row 4: Ch 1, sc in each st across, changing to victory red in last st, turn.

Row 5: Ch 1, sc in each st across, turn.

Rows 6–37: [Rep rows 2–5 consecutively] 8 times.

Rows 38 & 39: Rep rows 2 and 3.

Row 40: Ch 1, sc in each st across, turn.

Row 41: Holding first and last rows tog, matching sts, working through both thicknesses, ch 1, sc in each st across. Fasten off.

BAND
Rnd 1: Working in end of rows at one end of Sides, join dark royal with sc in any row, evenly sp 39 more sc around, join in beg sc. *(40 sc)*

Rnds 2–4: Ch 1, sc in each st around, join in beg sc.

Rnd 5: For **brim**, working this rnd in **front lps** *(see Stitch Guide)*, ch 1, hdc in first st, 2 hdc in next st, [hdc in next st, 2 hdc in next st] around, join in top of beg hdc. *(60 hdc)*

Rnd 6: Ch 1, hdc in each of first 4 sts, 2 hdc in next st, [hdc in each of next 4 sts, 2 hdc in next st] around, join in top of beg hdc. *(72 hdc)*

Rnd 7: Ch 1, hdc in each st around, join in top of beg hdc. Fasten off.

TOP

Rnd 1: With dark royal, ch 2, 5 sc in 2nd ch from hook, **do not join**. *(5 sc)*

Note: Do not join or turn rem rnds unless otherwise stated. Mark first st of each rnd.

Rnd 2: 2 sc in each st around. *(10 sc)*

Rnd 3: [Sc in next st, 2 sc in next st] around. *(15 sc)*

Rnd 4: [Sc in each of next 2 sts, 2 sc in next st] around. *(20 sc)*

Rnd 5: [Sc in each of next 3 sts, 2 sc in next st] around. *(25 sc)*

Rnd 6: [Sc in each of next 4 sts, 2 sc in next st] around. *(30 sc)*

Rnd 7: [Sc in each of next 5 sts, 2 sc in next st] around. *(35 sc)*

Rnd 8: [Sc in each of next 6 sts, 2 sc in next st] around, join in beg sc. Fasten off. *(40 sc)*

Easing to fit, sew Top to ends of rows at top of Hat.

With white, using **straight stitch** *(see Fig. 1)*, embroider 10 **starbursts** *(see Embroidery Diagram)* evenly spaced around Band of Hat. ■

Fig. 1
Straight Stitch

Starburst
Embroidery Diagram

Stitch Guide

For more complete information, visit **FreePatterns.com**

ABBREVIATIONS

beg	begin/begins/beginning
bpdc	back post double crochet
bpsc	back post single crochet
bptr	back post treble crochet
CC	contrasting color
ch(s)	chain(s)
ch-	refers to chain or space previously made (e.g., ch-1 space)
ch sp(s)	chain space(s)
cl(s)	cluster(s)
cm	centimeter(s)
dc	double crochet (singular/plural)
dc dec	double crochet 2 or more stitches together, as indicated
dec	decrease/decreases/decreasing
dtr	double treble crochet
ext	extended
fpdc	front post double crochet
fpsc	front post single crochet
fptr	front post treble crochet
g	gram(s)
hdc	half double crochet
hdc dec	half double crochet 2 or more stitches together, as indicated
inc	increase/increases/increasing
lp(s)	loop(s)
MC	main color
mm	millimeter(s)
oz	ounce(s)
pc	popcorn(s)
rem	remain/remains/remaining
rep(s)	repeat(s)
rnd(s)	round(s)
RS	right side
sc	single crochet (singular/plural)
sc dec	single crochet 2 or more stitches together, as indicated
sk	skip/skipped/skipping
sl st(s)	slip stitch(es)
sp(s)	space/spaces/spaced
st(s)	stitch(es)
tog	together
tr	treble crochet
trtr	triple treble
WS	wrong side
yd(s)	yard(s)
yo	yarn over

Chain—ch: Yo, pull through lp on hook.

Slip stitch—sl st: Insert hook in st, pull through both lps on hook.

Single crochet—sc: Insert hook in st, yo, pull through st, yo, pull through both lps on hook.

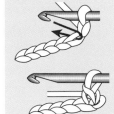

Front post stitch—fp: Back post stitch—bp: When working post st, insert hook from right to left around post st on previous row.

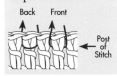

Back Front

Post of Stitch

Front loop—front lp Back loop—back lp

Front Loop   Back Loop

Half double crochet—hdc: Yo, insert hook in st, yo, pull through st, yo, pull through all 3 lps on hook.

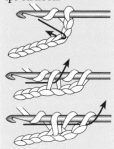

Double crochet—dc: Yo, insert hook in st, yo, pull through st, [yo, pull through 2 lps] twice.

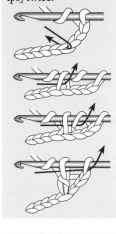

Change colors: Drop first color; with 2nd color, pull through last 2 lps of st.

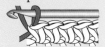

Treble crochet—tr: Yo twice, insert hook in st, yo, pull through st, [yo, pull through 2 lps] 3 times.

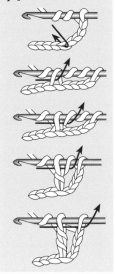

Double treble crochet—dtr: Yo 3 times, insert hook in st, yo, pull through st, [yo, pull through 2 lps] 4 times.

Single crochet decrease (sc dec): (Insert hook, yo, draw lp through) in each of the sts indicated, yo, draw through all lps on hook.

Example of 2-sc dec

Half double crochet decrease (hdc dec): (Yo, insert hook, yo, draw lp through) in each of the sts indicated, yo, draw through all lps on hook.

Example of 2-hdc dec

Double crochet decrease (dc dec): (Yo, insert hook, yo, draw loop through, draw through 2 lps on hook) in each of the sts indicated, yo, draw through all lps on hook.

Example of 2-dc dec

Treble crochet decrease (tr dec): Holding back last lp of each st, tr in each of the sts indicated, yo, pull through all lps on hook.

Example of 2-tr dec

US		UK
sl st (slip stitch)	=	sc (single crochet)
sc (single crochet)	=	dc (double crochet)
hdc (half double crochet)	=	htr (half treble crochet)
dc (double crochet)	=	tr (treble crochet)
tr (treble crochet)	=	dtr (double treble crochet)
dtr (double treble crochet)	=	ttr (triple treble crochet)
skip	=	miss

Metric
Conversion
Charts

METRIC CONVERSIONS

yards	x	.9144	=	metres (m)
yards	x	91.44	=	centimetres (cm)
inches	x	2.54	=	centimetres (cm)
inches	x	25.40	=	millimetres (mm)
inches	x	.0254	=	metres (m)

centimetres	x	.3937	=	inches
metres	x	1.0936	=	yards

INCHES INTO MILLIMETRES & CENTIMETRES (Rounded off slightly)

inches	mm	cm	inches	cm	inches	cm	inches	cm
1/8	3	0.3	5	12.5	21	53.5	38	96.5
1/4	6	0.6	5 1/2	14	22	56	39	99
3/8	10	1	6	15	23	58.5	40	101.5
1/2	13	1.3	7	18	24	61	41	104
5/8	15	1.5	8	20.5	25	63.5	42	106.5
3/4	20	2	9	23	26	66	43	109
7/8	22	2.2	10	25.5	27	68.5	44	112
1	25	2.5	11	28	28	71	45	114.5
1 1/4	32	3.2	12	30.5	29	73.5	46	117
1 1/2	38	3.8	13	33	30	76	47	119.5
1 3/4	45	4.5	14	35.5	31	79	48	122
2	50	5	15	38	32	81.5	49	124.5
2 1/2	65	6.5	16	40.5	33	84	50	127
3	75	7.5	17	43	34	86.5		
3 1/2	90	9	18	46	35	89		
4	100	10	19	48.5	36	91.5		
4 1/2	115	11.5	20	51	37	94		

KNITTING NEEDLES CONVERSION CHART

Canada/U.S.	0	1	2	3	4	5	6	7	8	9	10	10½	11	13	15
Metric (mm)	2	2¼	2¾	3¼	3½	3¾	4	4½	5	5½	6	6½	8	9	10

CROCHET HOOKS CONVERSION CHART

Canada/U.S.	1/B	2/C	3/D	4/E	5/F	6/G	8/H	9/I	10/J	10½/K	N
Metric (mm)	2.25	2.75	3.25	3.5	3.75	4.25	5	5.5	6	6.5	9.0

TOLL-FREE ORDER LINE or to request a free catalog (800) LV-ANNIE (800) 582-6643
Customer Service (800) AT-ANNIE (800) 282-6643, **Fax** (800) 882-6643
Visit AnniesAttic.com
We have made every effort to ensure the accuracy and completeness of these instructions.
We cannot, however, be responsible for human error, typographical mistakes or variations in individual work.

ISBN: 978-1-59635-285-8

1 2 3 4 5 6 7 8 9